973.2 Sam

W9-BNU-619

PRIMARY SOURCES OF EVERYDAY LIFE IN COLONIAL AMERICA™

Entertainment in Colonial America

Charlie Samuel

The Rosen Publishing Group's
PowerKids Press™
New York

Published in 2003 by The Rosen Publishing Group, Inc.
29 East 21st Street, New York, NY 10010

Photo Credits: Key: t: top, b: bottom, c: center, l: left, r: right
p.4t Corbis/Bettman; p.4b Mary Evans Picture Library; pp.7, 8, 11b Peter Newark's American Pictures; p.11tr Corbis/Hulton; p.12 AKG London; p.15t Corbis/Bettmann; p.15b Corbis/Historical Picture Archive; pp.16, 19tl Peter Newark's American Pictures; pp.19b, 20b Corbis/Bettmann; p.20tl AKG London; p.20tr Peter Newark's American Pictures.

Library of Congress Cataloging-in-Publication Data
Samuel, Charlie.
   Entertainment in colonial America / Charlie Samuel.
      v. cm. — (Primary sources of everyday life in colonial America)
Includes bibliographical references (p.) and index.
Contents: Life in a new land — Native American sports and games — Colonial sports — Games in the colonies — Music — Theater — Colonial stars — Social activities — Festivals — New kinds of entertainment.
   ISBN 0-8239-6600-3 (library binding)
   1. Recreation—United States—History—Colonial period, ca. 1600–1775—Juvenile literature. 2. Games—United States—History—Colonial period, ca. 1600–1775—Juvenile literature. 3. United States—Social life and customs—To 1775—Juvenile literature. [1. Recreation—History. 2. Games—History. 3. Sports—History. 4. United States—History—Colonial period, ca. 1600–1775. 5. United States—Social life and customs—To 1775.] I. Title. II. Series.
   GV53 .S26 2002
   790'.973'09033——dc21
                                                    2002004835

Contents

◄ This settlement on the New England coast has four cannons in the center of town. The lookout post on the hill was used by the settlers to guard against attacks by Native Americans.

▼ This is a walled English settlement in Carolina in 1675. The citizens of the town traded with native peoples and fished from their boats.

Life in a New Land

The first Europeans in America were Spaniards, who started to move to present-day Mexico after 1519, and to Florida after 1565. English settlers arrived on the East Coast in 1585 to create a settlement, or **colony**, at Roanoke. The French, Swedish, and Dutch also had begun colonies on the East Coast. By 1669, the English had taken over the Swedish and Dutch colonies. They claimed a total of 13 colonies along the coast from New Hampshire to Georgia. The French claimed land in what is now Canada. Later they claimed the land west of the Mississippi River.

By 1669, about 80,000 settlers lived in England's colonies. The population was growing quickly. The first settlers had struggled to find food and shelter, but life in colonies such as Massachusetts and Virginia was becoming easier. There were towns that had stores, churches, and schools. People had more free time to enjoy themselves. They wanted access to the same **luxuries** that people had in Europe.

Native American Sports and Games

The European colonists claimed American land without thinking about the fact that many Native American peoples already lived there. Some Native American groups attacked Europeans in an effort to protect their land. Other Native Americans welcomed the Europeans and helped them to survive in a new and different place.

Native Americans had their own sports and games. Many native groups held running races. **Archery** contests were also popular.

Among southeastern people, a popular sport was a ball game that was very similar to the modern game called lacrosse. The long playing field had a pole at each end. A team had at least 10 men, and each of them had two sticks. Both sticks had a small net at one end. The players used the sticks to catch and throw the ball. If the ball hit the pole, the attacking team scored a goal.

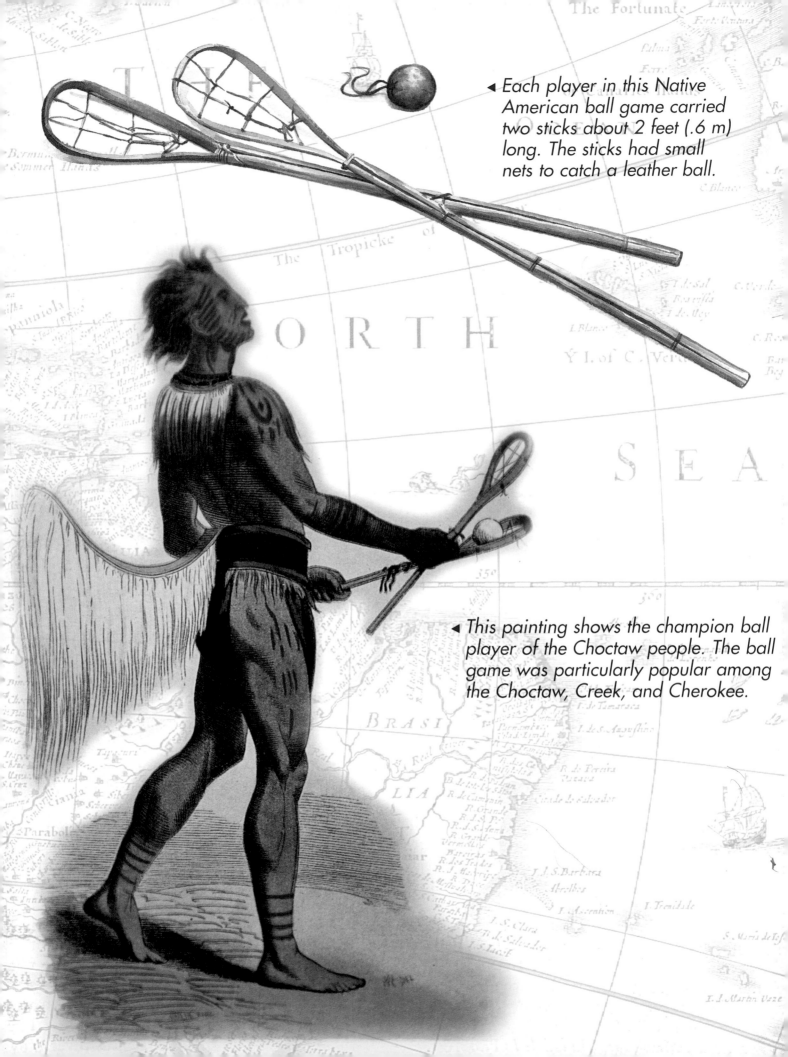

◄ Each player in this Native American ball game carried two sticks about 2 feet (.6 m) long. The sticks had small nets to catch a leather ball.

◄ This painting shows the champion ball player of the Choctaw people. The ball game was particularly popular among the Choctaw, Creek, and Cherokee.

► This picture shows George Washington, the first president of the United States, hunting for foxes.

▼ This notice told people about a horse race in 1776. Horse racing was especially popular among Dutch colonists.

LONG-ISLAND HORSE RACE.

TO be run for, on Thursday the 6th of November next, at the New Lots, on Long-Island, about seven miles from Brooklyn ferry, a PURSE, value ONE HUNDRED DOLLARS, or upwards, by three years old colts or fillies, the best of three heats, one mile to each heat; three quarter blood carrying eight stone, half blood seven stone nine pounds, &c. &c.——All horses running for the above purse to pay one guinea entrance; which money will be run for the next day by all except the winning horse the first day.

PUBLIC AUCTION.

ON Monday morning, 11 o'clock, at the coffee-house, will be sold, a fine large black horse, only 5 years old, fit either for saddle or chair.

On Tuesday, a quantity of Barcelona wine in

Colonial Sports

The English played many sports. Colonists played the same sports in America. Some sports were very old, such as archery or hunting on horseback. Sports were good ways for people to practice skills that were useful in the **militia**, such as horse riding. Other popular sports were tennis, a game similar to baseball called rounders, and a game like soccer. In the French colony in Canada, people played ice hockey. Some colonists liked to play golf, which came from Scotland. One of the most popular sports was fishing, because it provided food.

In the late 1600s, wealthy citizens in Virginia brought horses from England for racing. Dutch colonists, in particular, enjoyed horse races. Many **Puritans** protested horse racing, because people bet on which horse they thought would win. Puritans thought gambling was a sin.

◄ *Celebrating Christmas was not accepted in New England until about 1875. Puritans did not believe in or celebrate Christmas. Here a Puritan minister scolds some townspeople for celebrating the holiday.*

Games in the Colonies

The games that colonists played were like the games that people played in England. Children, for example, rolled wooden hoops and played leapfrog and hopscotch. They also played marbles and flew homemade kites. Adults played quoits, which was like playing horseshoes today. Not everyone enjoyed such games, however. Some church leaders thought that games should be limited. They thought that working was more important than playing, because work was done in the service of God. No games were allowed on Sunday, which was considered holy and was reserved for going to church.

Other **pastimes** that came from Europe were more cruel. Settlers enjoyed cockfighting, in which two roosters fought each other until one was killed. Another cruel game involved pulling on a goose in a tug-of-war. Men also enjoyed games in **taverns**, such as **bowls**, **skittles**, and darts. They played card games, such as poker, for money.

▶ *Men made bets as they watched cockfights. The roosters were bred to fight. The contest finished only when one rooster was killed by the other.*

▼ *Men enjoy a game of bowls outside a tavern. Like other colonial games, bowls originally came from Europe.*

This is a portrait of the eighteenth-century German composer George Frederick Handel. Handel's music became popular in America among amateur musicians.

This illustration for the music of "Yankee Doodle" shows a drummer and piper from the American Revolution, which began in 1775. American soldiers either sang or played the song as they marched.

Yankee Doodle

Father and I went down to camp, A-long with Captain Goodwin

And there we saw the men and boys As thick as hast-ty pud-ding

Yan-kee doo-dle keep it up. Yan-kee doo-dle dan-dy,

Mind the mu-sic and the step, And with the girls be han-dy.

Music

There was not much music in the early colonies. Groups such as the Puritans thought that music took people's attention away from **worship**. The Puritans sang hymns without music. Until 1721, their hymns did not even have tunes. Each singer made up his or her own tune.

By the late seventeenth century there was more music in the colonies. Families sang and played fiddles, banjos, and flutes. The tune of "Yankee Doodle," which is still popular today, was first written in 1715 as a nursery song. It later became popular as a soldiers' marching song.

In the early eighteenth century, musicians began to perform work by European **composers** such as Johann Sebastian Bach and George Frederick Handel. The first classical music concert took place in 1731, and the first music college opened in Pennsylvania around the same time.

African slaves made up songs to sing while they worked. These songs were the start of forms of music such as gospel and the blues.

Theater

Many people thought that theaters encouraged poor morals. Many colonies banned theaters and acting, but settlers sometimes put on plays in their homes.

The first public plays began in 1700, when an actor named Richard Hunter got a **license** to perform in New York. English actors soon began to tour the colonies. They often acted in hotels or barns to get around rules that banned theaters.

The first real theater in the colonies opened in Williamsburg, Virginia, in 1717. It soon closed but another took its place in 1752. Other theaters followed in places such as New York, Annapolis, and Charleston.

Most theaters in the colonies staged English plays, such as the works of William Shakespeare. It wasn't until 1767 that the Southwark Theater in Philadelphia put on the first play written in America, *The Prince of Parthia* by Thomas Godfrey.

► This advertisement for a play includes part of the script. The play was performed in a hotel in Charlestown in 1735.

Prologue spoken to the ORPHAN, upon it's being play'd at Charlestown, on Tuesday the 24th of Jan. 1734-5.

WHen first Columbus touch'd this distant Shore,
And vainly hop'd his Fears and Dangers o'er,
One boundless Wilderness in View appear'd!
No Champain Plains or rising Cities chear'd
His wearied Eye. ———
Monsters unknown travers'd the hideous Waste,
And Men more Savage than the Beasts they chac'd.
But mark! how soon these gloomy Prospects clear,
And the new World's late horrors disappear.
The soil obedient to the industrious Swains,
With happy Harvests crowns their honest Pains,
And Peace and Plenty triumph o'er the Plains.
What various Products float on every Tide!
What numerous Navys in our Harbours ride!
Tillage and Trade conjoin their Friendly Aid,
T'enrich the thriving Boy and lovely Maid.
Hispania, it's true, her precious Mines engross'd,
And bore her shining Entrails to its Coast.
Britannia more humane supplys her wants,
The Brittish Sense and Brittish Beauty plants.
The Aged Sire beholds with sweet Surprize
In foreign Climes a numerous Offspring rize.
Sense, Virtue, worth and Honour stand confest,
In each brave Male, his prosp'rous hands have blest,
While the admiring Eye improv'd may trace
The Mother's Charms in each chast Virgins Face.
Hence we presume to usher in those Arts
Which oft have warm'd the best and bravest Hearts
Faints our endeavours, rude are our Essays;
We strive to please, but can't pretend at praise;
Forgiving Smiles o'erpay the grateful Task;
They're all we hope and all we humbly ask.

At the right of this engraving of Philadelphia stands the New Theater, which was built in the mid-eighteenth century.

▼ The theater was thought to encourage wicked behavior. Before proper theaters were allowed, performances were held in other places. Here, actors change in a barn before a performance.

THE LYING VALET;
A FARCE, IN TWO ACTS.—BY D. GARRICK.

Act II. Scene I.

CHARACTERS.

GAYLESS	BEAU TRIPPET	MRS. GADABOUT
SHARP	DRUNKEN COOK	MRS. TRIPPET
JUSTICE GUTTLE	MELISSA	KITTY PRY

◄ This advertisement announced a performance of The Lying Valet. The play was staged at the Southwark Theater in Philadelphia in October 1773.

▼ An actress named Mrs. Pownall, shown wearing a stage costume in this drawing, was famous at the time of the American Revolution.

▼ John Hodgkinson became a famous actor in the late colonial period.

Colonial Stars

In 1749, the English actors William Murray and Thomas Kean led a theater group on a tour of the American colonies. The tour helped to make plays more popular. Three years later Charles and Mary Stagg built a new theater in Williamsburg, Virginia. They brought an actor called Lewis Hallam and his family from England to perform. The Hallam family were a great success in Williamsburg for many years. They later toured the colonies.

In the last decades of the colonial period, some actors and actresses became extremely popular. The stars included the Hallams and other English performers, and Americans such as John Hodgkinson and Mrs. Pownall.

Musicians were also popular. Some became famous even though playing music was not really their job. Sy Gilliat, for example, was a slave who belonged to the governor of Virginia. Sy was a fine fiddler. He was often asked to play at dances in the neighborhood.

Social Activities

In the early years of the colonies people were too busy to **socialize** often. People met up with their neighbors at church or at events such as weddings. Sometimes communities also got together to share large tasks, such as building a new barn.

As the colonies grew richer and life grew easier, people had more time to relax. Many events were still based around doing something useful, however. At a quilting **bee**, for example, women and girls visited together to make warm, decorative blankets.

Men met their friends at inns and taverns to drink and play games. Wealthy men sometimes held large dinners, or feasts, to mark important **civic** events.

Wealthy families often visited each other's homes to make music or to act in plays. By the middle of the eighteenth century, however, **audiences** could enjoy more plays and concerts performed by **professionals**.

This Evening,

The Tenth of *December*, at Six o'Clock, the

NEW
ORGAN,

At KING'S CHURCH, will be play'd on by Mr. FLAGG.

A Number of Gentlemen belonging to the Town will affift on the Occafion, and perform the vocal Parts. A SERMON, on the Lawfulnefs, Excellency and Advantage of INSTRUMENTAL MUSIC in public Worfhip, will be preached by the Reverend JOHN GRAVES, after which a Collection will be made to defray the Expence of bringing the ORGAN from *Bofton*, and fixing it in the Church.

"*Praife him with ORGANS.*"---Pfalm cl. 4.

"*Praise him with danceing and the Stringed Instruments Pfm. 150. 4.*"

◄ This advertisement announced a concert to be played on a new organ at King's Church in Providence, Rhode Island, in the eighteenth century. There would also be a sermon about music. The church played an important part in social life during the whole colonial period.

▼ At a quilting bee, women and girls got together to share their work and to swap stories.

A MAIN and several MATCHES, AT DYDE'S Mount Vernon Hotel, On the Turf, If the weather will permit, or otherwise in a large room, On Friday the 17th....St.Patrick's Day. Commences at 11o'clock. An Excellent Dinner Will be set on the Table at 1 o'clock, at 6 shillings each, drinkables included. SOUTHWICK.....SUE, PRINTERS, No. 2, WALL-STREET.

▲ This advertisement in an eighteenth-century New York newspaper announces a cockfight to celebrate Saint Patrick's Day.

◄ This German family is celebrating Saint Nicholas Day on December 6.

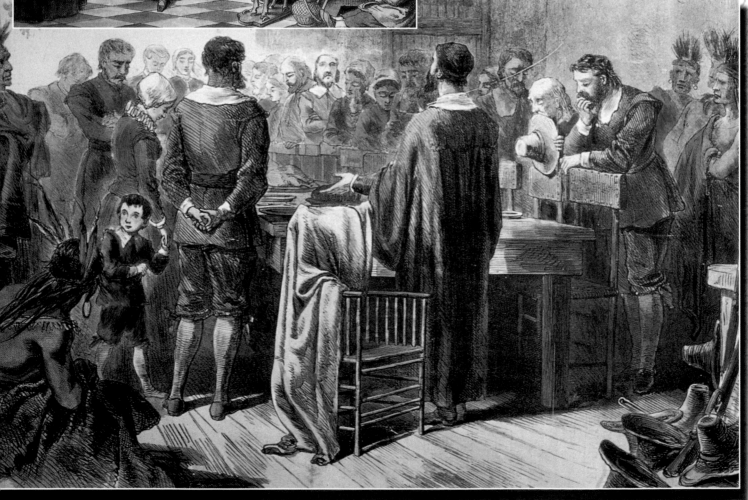

Festivals

Festivals were special days when people could enjoy themselves. Some holidays were religious, such as Christmas and Easter. Dutch and German colonists celebrated Saint Nicholas Day on December 6. In the French and Spanish colonies, people held a **carnival** before **Lent**, the time before Easter when some Christians try to give up something that they enjoy.

Other celebrations related to the passing year. May Day, for example, marked the start of spring. People danced around a maypole. After 1621, the custom grew of holding a feast called Thanksgiving in the fall to give thanks for the harvest. Thanksgiving remains an important holiday today. Native Americans celebrated a midwinter ceremony.

Other festivals were linked to events. Muster Day, when the militia gathered to train, was a major holiday, as was Election Day. Almost any unusual event, even a funeral, attracted crowds.

◄ *This drawing shows Thanksgiving in 1621. It is believed that the Puritans invited their Native American neighbors to celebrate the harvest.*

New Kinds of Entertainment

By the middle of the 1700s, life in the colonies was very different from how it had been before. People enjoyed new pastimes. There were more theaters, where people could watch new plays written by Americans, not only by English writers from the past. Music societies in a number of cities encouraged the first American composers of classical music, too. William Billings became particularly well-known for writing popular songs. John Frederick Peter composed music for the pipe organ.

Reading was a popular pastime. Philadelphia alone had 77 bookshops that sold novels, plays, poems, and news of events. Almost every colony had at least one **printing press**.

Books were very important in spreading the ideas that led to the start of the American Revolution in 1775. The colonies wanted to govern themselves. Eight years later the colonies defeated the English and created the United States.

Glossary

archery (AR-chur-ee) A sport in which players use a bow to shoot arrows at a target.

audiences (AW-dee-ens-ez) Groups of people who listen to or watch something.

bee (BEE) A social group that meets for a specific purpose.

bowls (BOHLZ) A game in which players roll balls as close as they can to a target ball called a jack.

carnival (KAR-nih-vul) A public celebration with food, music, dancing, and other entertainment.

civic (SIH-vik) Having to do with a city, a citizen, or citizenship.

colony (KAH-luh-nee) A new place where people live, but where they are still ruled by their old country's leaders.

composers (kom-POH-zerz) People who write and create music.

Lent (LENT) A period of 40 days before Easter when some Christians try to give up something they enjoy.

license (LY-sins) Official permission to do something.

luxuries (LUK-shreez) Things that are enjoyable but that are not necessary.

militia (muh-LIH-shuh) A group of people who are trained and ready to fight in an emergency.

pastimes (PAS-tymz) Hobbies or activities that make time pass in an enjoyable way.

printing press (PRINT-ing PRESS) A machine used to print many copies of something.

professionals (pruh-FEH-shuh-nulz) People who do something very well and are paid to do it.

Puritans (PYUR-ih-tinz) People in the 1500s and 1600s who belonged to the Protestant religion.

skittles (SKIH-tulz) A game in which players roll a ball to knock down pins.

socialize (SOH-shul-eyz) To seek out the company of others.

taverns (TA-vurnz) Places to spend the evening or eat a meal.

worship (WUR-ship) Prayer, religious services, and other acts done in honor of God or a god.

Index

Primary Sources

Page 4 (bottom). Engraving of a settlement in Carolina, 1675. **Page 8 (top left).** Advertisement for horse race printed in Rivington's *Gazette*, New York, October 17, 1776. **Page 11 (top).** The cockfighting picture is an engraving made by the English artist William Hogarth around 1760. **Page 12 (top).** This portrait of George Frederick Handel is a copy made in 1748 of a picture painted by Philippe Mercier in the 1720s. **Page 15 (top right).** Theater notice from a Charleston newspaper, 1735. **Page 15 (bottom).** *Strolling Actresses in a Barn* is a print based on a 1738 painting by the English artist William Hogarth, who intended to show the immorality of the theater. **Page 16 (top left).** Playbill for *The Lying Valet* at the Southwark Theater, Philadelphia, October 1773, from Peter Newark's American Pictures. **Page 19 (top).** Eighteenth-century advertisement for a new organ at the King's Church, Providence, Rhode Island. **Page 20 (top right).** Eighteenth-century advertisement from a New York newspaper for a cockfight and dinner to celebrate Saint Patrick's Day.

Web Sites

Due to the changing nature of Internet links, PowerKids Press has developed an online list of Web sites related to the subject of this book. This site is updated regularly. Please use this link to access the list: www.powerkidslinks.com/pselca/entca

Colonial Stars

In 1749, the English actors William Murray and Thomas Kean led a theater group on a tour of the American colonies. The tour helped to make plays more popular. Three years later Charles and Mary Stagg built a new theater in Williamsburg, Virginia. They brought an actor called Lewis Hallam and his family from England to perform. The Hallam family were a great success in Williamsburg for many years. They later toured the colonies.

In the last decades of the colonial period, some actors and actresses became extremely popular. The stars included the Hallams and other English performers, and Americans such as John Hodgkinson and Mrs. Pownall.

Musicians were also popular. Some became famous even though playing music was not really their job. Sy Gilliat, for example, was a slave who belonged to the governor of Virginia. Sy was a fine fiddler. He was often asked to play at dances in the neighborhood.

Social Activities

In the early years of the colonies people were too busy to **socialize** often. People met up with their neighbors at church or at events such as weddings. Sometimes communities also got together to share large tasks, such as building a new barn.

As the colonies grew richer and life grew easier, people had more time to relax. Many events were still based around doing something useful, however. At a quilting **bee**, for example, women and girls visited together to make warm, decorative blankets.

Men met their friends at inns and taverns to drink and play games. Wealthy men sometimes held large dinners, or feasts, to mark important **civic** events.

Wealthy families often visited each other's homes to make music or to act in plays. By the middle of the eighteenth century, however, **audiences** could enjoy more plays and concerts performed by **professionals**.

This Evening,

The Tenth of *December*, at Six o'Clock, the

NEW

ORGAN,

At King's Church, will be play'd on by Mr. Flagg.

A Number of Gentlemen belonging to the Town will assist on the Occasion, and perform the vocal Parts. A SERMON, on the Lawfulness, Excellency and Advantage of INSTRUMENTAL MUSIC in public Worship, will be preached by the Reverend JOHN GRAVES, after which a Collection will be made to defray the Expence of bringing the ORGAN from *Boston*, and fixing it in the Church.

" *Praise him with ORGANS.* "---Psalm cl. 4.

" *Praise him with danceing and the Stringed Instruments Psm 150. 4th.* "

◄ This advertisement announced a concert to be played on a new organ at King's Church in Providence, Rhode Island, in the eighteenth century. There would also be a sermon about music. The church played an important part in social life during the whole colonial period.

▼ At a quilting bee, women and girls got together to share their work and to swap stories.

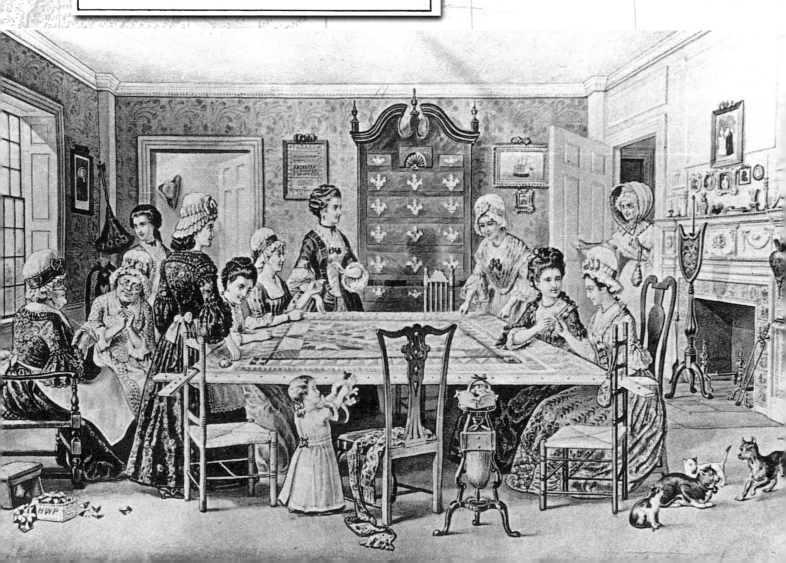

▲ This advertisement in an eighteenth-century New York newspaper announces a cockfight to celebrate Saint Patrick's Day.

◄ This German family is celebrating Saint Nicholas Day on December 6.

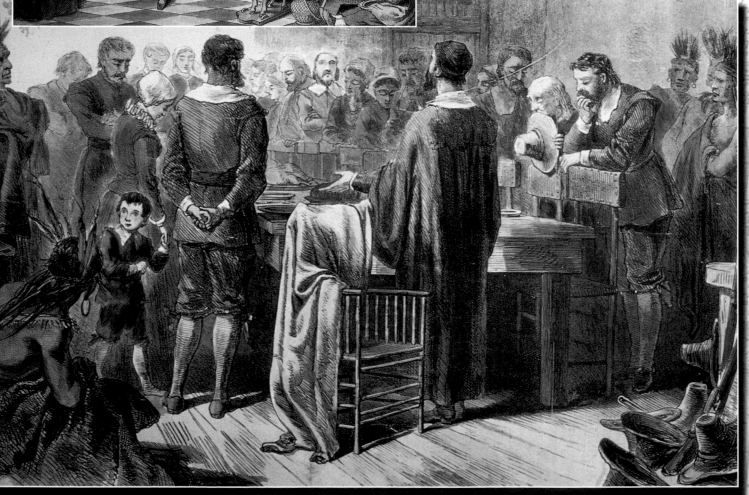

Festivals

Festivals were special days when people could enjoy themselves. Some holidays were religious, such as Christmas and Easter. Dutch and German colonists celebrated Saint Nicholas Day on December 6. In the French and Spanish colonies, people held a **carnival** before **Lent**, the time before Easter when some Christians try to give up something that they enjoy.

Other celebrations related to the passing year. May Day, for example, marked the start of spring. People danced around a maypole. After 1621, the custom grew of holding a feast called Thanksgiving in the fall to give thanks for the harvest. Thanksgiving remains an important holiday today. Native Americans celebrated a midwinter ceremony.

Other festivals were linked to events. Muster Day, when the militia gathered to train, was a major holiday, as was Election Day. Almost any unusual event, even a funeral, attracted crowds.

◄ *This drawing shows Thanksgiving in 1621. It is believed that the Puritans invited their Native American neighbors to celebrate the harvest.*

New Kinds of Entertainment

By the middle of the 1700s, life in the colonies was very different from how it had been before. People enjoyed new pastimes. There were more theaters, where people could watch new plays written by Americans, not only by English writers from the past. Music societies in a number of cities encouraged the first American composers of classical music, too. William Billings became particularly well-known for writing popular songs. John Frederick Peter composed music for the pipe organ.

Reading was a popular pastime. Philadelphia alone had 77 bookshops that sold novels, plays, poems, and news of events. Almost every colony had at least one **printing press**.

Books were very important in spreading the ideas that led to the start of the American Revolution in 1775. The colonies wanted to govern themselves. Eight years later the colonies defeated the English and created the United States.

Glossary

archery (AR-chur-ee) A sport in which players use a bow to shoot arrows at a target.

audiences (AW-dee-ens-ez) Groups of people who listen to or watch something.

bee (BEE) A social group that meets for a specific purpose.

bowls (BOHLZ) A game in which players roll balls as close as they can to a target ball called a jack.

carnival (KAR-nih-vul) A public celebration with food, music, dancing, and other entertainment.

civic (SIH-vik) Having to do with a city, a citizen, or citizenship.

colony (KAH-luh-nee) A new place where people live, but where they are still ruled by their old country's leaders.

composers (kom-POH-zerz) People who write and create music.

Lent (LENT) A period of 40 days before Easter when some Christians try to give up something they enjoy.

license (LY-sins) Official permission to do something.

luxuries (LUK-shreez) Things that are enjoyable but that are not necessary.

militia (muh-LIH-shuh) A group of people who are trained and ready to fight in an emergency.

pastimes (PAS-tymz) Hobbies or activities that make time pass in an enjoyable way.

printing press (PRINT-ing PRESS) A machine used to print many copies of something.

professionals (pruh-FEH-shuh-nulz) People who do something very well and are paid to do it.

Puritans (PYUR-ih-tinz) People in the 1500s and 1600s who belonged to the Protestant religion.

skittles (SKIH-tulz) A game in which players roll a ball to knock down pins.

socialize (SOH-shul-eyz) To seek out the company of others.

taverns (TA-vurnz) Places to spend the evening or eat a meal.

worship (WUR-ship) Prayer, religious services, and other acts done in honor of God or a god.

Index

Primary Sources

Page 4 (bottom). Engraving of a settlement in Carolina, 1675. **Page 8 (top left).** Advertisement for horse race printed in Rivington's *Gazette*, New York, October 17, 1776. **Page 11 (top).** The cockfighting picture is an engraving made by the English artist William Hogarth around 1760. **Page 12 (top).** This portrait of George Frederick Handel is a copy made in 1748 of a picture painted by Philippe Mercier in the 1720s. **Page 15 (top right).** Theater notice from a Charleston newspaper, 1735. **Page 15 (bottom).** *Strolling Actresses in a Barn* is a print based on a 1738 painting by the English artist William Hogarth, who intended to show the immorality of the theater. **Page 16 (top left).** Playbill for *The Lying Valet* at the Southwark Theater, Philadelphia, October 1773, from Peter Newark's American Pictures. **Page 19 (top).** Eighteenth-century advertisement for a new organ at the King's Church, Providence, Rhode Island. **Page 20 (top right).** Eighteenth-century advertisement from a New York newspaper for a cockfight and dinner to celebrate Saint Patrick's Day.

Web Sites

Due to the changing nature of Internet links, PowerKids Press has developed an online list of Web sites related to the subject of this book. This site is updated regularly. Please use this link to access the list: www.powerkidslinks.com/pselca/entca